FEAST OF BOOTHS BIRTH OF JESUS 8 B.C.
Copyright © 2023 by Douglas Wayne Ophus
All rights reserved by the publisher, except as permitted under U. S. Copyright Act of 1976.

Unless otherwise noted scriptures are from the New King James Version (Nashville: Thomas Nelson Inc., 1982)

Other scriptures quoted
Holman Christian Standard Bible (Nashville: Holman Bible Publishers, 2003)

The NKJV Greek English Interlinear New Testament (Nashville: Thomas Nelson Publishers, 1994)

Published by
FUTURE HISTORY BEFORE IT HAPPENS BOOKS LLC
www.futurehistorybeforeithappensbooks.com

Library of Congress Cataloging-in-Publication Data
Ophus, Douglas Wayne
FEAST OF BOOTHS BIRTH OF JESUS 8 B.C.

ISBN-13: 979-8-218-16958-9
Printed in the United States of America

Introduction
This book calculates from the course of Abijah that Zachariah served in 9 B.C. to the Feast of Booths in 8 B.C. when Jesus was born. The Feast of booths is a celebration foreshadowing the birth of the Messiah, who is Jesus. It is necessary that the Feast of Booths pertain to the Messiah because there are Burnt-Offerings made by the residents to the Lord. Furthermore, the residents themselves make the Burnt-Offerings, which speak of Justification directly to the Lord without intervening priests doing it. This book demonstrates that God is true to His word and it upholds the veracity of Luke.
Douglas W. Ophus, BA, MA, Theological Studies

The Feast of Booths

The Feast of Booths and Tabernacles is a very joyful celebration that symbolically foreshadows the birth of the Messiah.

Many of the other feast days, also symbolically foreshadow aspects of the work of the Messiah, who we now know to be Jesus.

The year Jesus was born according to Luke

Having the advantage of other studies that have gone before me and my own studies, I have become convinced that Jesus was born in the year of the census of Caesar Augustus that we date as 8 B.C. In fact, Luke is quite clear about it.

(Luke 2:1)
And it came to pass in those days *that* a decree went out from Caesar Augustus that all the world should be registered.
(Luke 2:2)
This registration was former of Quirinius governing Syria.
(Luke 2:2 is Author's translation, see pp. 51-55)

There was a Caesar Augustus census that we date as 8 B.C. Julian and one that we date as 14 A.D. Julian. Quirinius is best known to have been Legate, 'governor' of Syria from 6 to 7 A.D., at

3

which time he carried out a census that included Judaea. He continued as Legate until 12 A.D.; therefore, with this translation, Luke is saying that it was the earlier one, the one before Quirinius was governor of Syria. (See end notes for 8 B.C. census)

Comparing the Feast of Booths and Tabernacles to the birth of Jesus

The first place that booths appear in the Bible is as an animal shelter

The first-place sukkot (or succoth) 'booths' appears in the Bible is in Genesis 33:17.
17 **And Jacob journeyed to Succoth, built himself a house, and made booths for his livestock. Therefore the name of the place is called Succoth.**

Three-sided sukkot 'booths' (plural of sukkah) would be appropriate animal pens for livestock such as sheep and goats in a warm climate because in a completely enclosed structure the livestock would get too hot and might get sick.

The Feast of Booths and Tabernacles as given by God to Moses that he told to the people of Israel is in Leviticus 23:33-44

33 **Then the Lord spoke to Moses, saying.** 34 "Speak to the children of Israel, saying: 'The fifteenth day of this seventh month *shall be* the Feast of Tabernacles *for* seven days to the Lord. 35 On the first day *there shall be* a holy convocation. You shall do no customary work *on it.* 36 *For* seven days you shall offer an offering made by fire to the Lord. On the eighth day you shall have a holy convocation, and you shall offer an offering made by fire to the Lord. It *is* a sacred assembly, *and* you shall do no customary work *on it.* 37 'These *are* the feasts of the Lord which you shall proclaim *to be* holy convocations, to offer an offering made by fire to the Lord, a burnt offering and a grain offering, a sacrifice and drink offerings, everything on its day—38 besides the Sabbaths of the Lord, besides your gifts, besides all your vows, and besides all your freewill offerings which you give to the Lord. 39 'Also on the fifteenth day of the seventh month, when you have gathered in the fruit of the land, you shall keep the feast of the Lord *for* seven days; on the first day *there shall be* a sabbath-*rest,* and on the eighth day a sabbath-*rest.*

40 And you shall take for yourselves on the first day the fruit of beautiful trees, branches of palm trees, the boughs of leafy trees, and willows of the brook; and you shall rejoice before the Lord

your God for seven days. 41 You shall keep it as a feast to the Lord for seven days in the year. *It shall be* a statute forever in your generations. You shall celebrate it in the seventh month. 42 You shall dwell in booths for seven days. All who are native Israelites shall dwell in booths, 43 that your generations may know that I made the children of Israel dwell in booths when I brought them out of the land of Egypt: I *am* the Lord your God.'" 44 So Moses declared to the children of Israel the feasts of the Lord.

Luke describes Joseph and Mary traveling from their home in Nazareth to Bethlehem in order to register, and while they were there in Bethlehem, Jesus was born.

Luke 2:3-7
3 So all went to be registered, everyone to his own city. 4 Joseph also went up from Galilee, out of the city of Nazareth, into Judea, to the city of David, which is called Bethlehem, because he was of the house and lineage of David, 5 to be registered with Mary, his betrothed wife, who was with child. 6 So it was that while they were there, the days were completed for her to be delivered. 7 And she brought forth her firstborn Son, and wrapped Him in swaddling cloths, and laid Him in a manger, because there was no room for them in the inn.

The birth of Jesus fulfilled the foreshadowing of the birth of the Messiah that is symbolized in the Feast of Booths and Tabernacles

The Feast of Booths begins on Tishri 15 on the Jewish calendar. In 8 B.C., Tishri 15 began on October 20, a Monday. A new Jewish day begins after sunset. So, in 8 B.C. the Feast of Booths began after sunset on Sunday evening.

Luke 2:7 says that they laid Him in a manger. That speaks of Jesus being born in an animal pen or booth such as is celebrated during the Feast of Booths and Tabernacles.

In Luke 2:8-20 an angel of the Lord appeared to shepherds that were tending their flocks by night. The angel stood before the shepherds and the glory of the Lord shown around them, then the angel told them that there is born to you this day in the city of David, a Savior, who is Christ the Lord. A sign to them will be that they will find a baby in a manger. They decide to go to Bethlehem and see the thing the Lord has brought to pass.
The Angel appeared to the shepherds as they were tending their flocks, after sunset, and the angel spoke of Jesus having been born this day.
So, Jesus was born on Sunday after sunset.

The shepherds that went to see Jesus on the first day of the Feast of Booths were part of the holy convocation on the first day spoken of in Lev. 23:3

Lev. 23:40 speaks of taking fruit, branches of palm trees, boughs of leafy trees, and willows on the first day. (Traditionally these are placed on the roof of the booth). During the triumphal entry of Jesus into Jerusalem, many people took branches of palm trees and went to meet him as described in John 12:13.

In Lev. 23:40, they were to rejoice for seven days. In Luke 2:10, an angel told the shepherds, **"Do not be afraid, for behold, I bring you good tidings of great joy which will be to all people."**

In Lev 23:36, on the eighth day there is to be another holy convocation. In Luke 2:21, on the eighth day they brought Jesus to be circumcised.

Luke 2:21
21 **And when eight days were completed for the circumcision of the Child, His name was called Jesus, the name given by the angel before He was conceived in the womb.**

They remained there and did not go to Jerusalem until after Mary was purified according to the law of Moses.

Luke 2:22-24

22 **Now when the days of her purification according to the law of Moses were completed, they brought Him to Jerusalem to present** *Him* **to the Lord 23 (as it is written in the law of the Lord,** *"Every male who opens the womb shall be called holy to the Lord"***), 24 and to offer a sacrifice according to what is said in the law of the Lord,** *"A pair of turtledoves or two young pigeons."*

Luke 2:39

39 **So when they had performed all things according to the law of the Lord, they returned to Galilee, to their** *own* **city Nazareth.**

The conception of John and Jesus

When Elizabeth, the mother of John the Baptist, conceived John in her womb is information that facilitates determining when Mary, the mother of Jesus, conceived Jesus in her womb. Elizabeth was exactly six months pregnant with John when Mary conceived Jesus in her womb by the power of the Holy Spirit.

Luke 1:5-13

5 There was in the days of Herod, the king of Judea, a certain priest named Zacharias, of the division of Abijah. His wife *was* of the daughters of Aaron, and her name *was* Elizabeth. 6 And they were both righteous before God, walking in all the commandments and ordinances of the Lord blameless. 7 But they had no child, because Elizabeth was barren, and they were both well advanced in years. 8 So it was that while he was serving as priest before God in the order of his division, 9 according to the custom of the priesthood, his lot fell to burn incense when he went into the temple of the Lord. 10 And the whole multitude of the people was praying outside at the hour of incense. 11 Then an angel of the Lord appeared to him, standing on the right side of the altar of incense. 12 And when Zacharias saw *him*, he was troubled, and fear fell upon him. 13 But the angel said to him, "Do not be afraid, Zacharias, for your prayer is heard; and your wife Elizabeth will bear you a son, and you shall call his name John.

1:18-20 Zachariah expressed doubt because of their age. Gabriel replied, "You will be mute and not able to speak until the day these things take place because you did not believe my words which will be fulfilled in their own time."

10

Luke states that Zachariah of the division of Abijah, who was the husband of Elizabeth, was serving as a priest in the Temple when an angel appeared to him, saying, **"Your prayer has been heard."** εἰσηκούσθη 'has been heard' is an aorist one indictive passive (completed action is meant). They were having sexual relations in an attempt to conceive a child without success and were even brought to the point of needing to pray to have the child. Their prayer has been heard. Now, divine providence and power has been made known by the angel Gabriel, and now, it is at work. Their child was an answer to prayer and at the time of the announcement of the angel, John was conceived in Elizabeth's womb. That could be explained by lingering sperm that was allowed to conceive John at the appointed time announced by the angel. We know today that it is possible for sperm to linger for some time.

Luke 1:23
Καὶ ἐγένετο ὡς ἐπλήσθησαν
And it was as were fulfilled

αἱ ἡμέραι τῆς λειτουργίας αὐτοῦ
the days of the of service of him

ἀπῆλθεν εἰς τὸν οἶκον αὐτοῦ
he went away into the house of him

The reason for referring to the Greek Text is to demonstrate that when the angel appeared to Zachariah, it was on the forenoon of the second Sabbath of the course of Abijah. That is because as Zachariah came out of the Temple his course of service was over and he went home. ἐπλήσθησαν is a 3rd person plural aorist indicative passive; the plural aorist form indicates that *all* was completed. Verse 1:24, After John was conceived in Elizabeth, she hid herself for five months; however, that does not enter into the calculation of when Jesus was conceived in Mary.

Luke 1:26-27
26 Now in the sixth month the angel Gabriel was sent by God to a city of Galilee named Nazareth, 27 to a virgin betrothed to a man whose name was Joseph, of the house of David. The virgin's name was Mary.
Luke 1:30-31
30 Then the angel said to her, "Do not be afraid, Mary, for you have found favor with God. 31 And behold, you will conceive in your womb and bring forth a son, and shall call His name Jesus."
Luke 1:36-37
36 "Now indeed, Elizabeth your relative has also conceived a son in her old age; and this is now the sixth month for her who was called barren. 37 For with God nothing will be impossible.

Mary visits Elizabeth

Luke 1:39-41 And Mary rose up in these days and went into the hill country with haste to a city in Judah, then she entered the house of Zachariah and greeted Elizabeth. When Elizabeth heard Mary's voice, baby John leaped in her womb and Elizabeth was filled with the Holy Spirit.

Luke 1:56 Mary stayed with Elizabeth about three months before returning to her house.

(6 plus 3 months equals 9 months so, Marry most likely stayed with Elizabeth until John was born. In that case, Mary would have been a witness to the events that occurred at the time of the birth of John. When Zachariah wrote his name is John, and then Zachariah's speech was restored, Luke 1:57-79.)

Zachariah was not the High Priest and he was not serving on the Day of Atonement

Some have suggested that Zachariah was the High Priest and that he was serving on the Day of Atonement when the angel appeared to him. Luke 1:9 says that Zachariah's lot fell to serve incense. The High Priest was not chosen by lot to serve incense on the Day of Atonement; he served on the Day of Atonement because that was his duty.

In Luke 1:23, Zachariah went into his house.

In Luke 1:39-40, Zachariah lived in a city in the hill country of Judah. So, Zachariah's house was not in Jerusalem. Since the High Priest lived in Jerusalem, Zachariah was not the High Priest.

Knowing the date that the course of Abijah served when John was conceived in Elizabeth would facilitate determining when Jesus was conceived in Mary. Luke states that Elizabeth, the mother of John the Baptist, was six months pregnant with John when the angel spoke to Mary, the mother of Jesus; and at that very time, Jesus was conceived in Mary's womb by the power of the Holy Spirit while Mary remained a virgin.

The course of Abijah is number eight

King David of Israel wanted to build a Temple of the Lord. However, God did not desire that he should be the one to build the Temple since he had shed blood. The actual building of the Temple would be done by David's son, Solomon. David drew plans for the Temple and he organized the priests into twenty-four courses. Then they drew lots to determine the place in the order that each course should serve. The division of Abijah drew number eight. The drawing of lots is given in first Chronicles 24:1-19.

Calculating the days and dates between when the course of Abijah served in 9 B.C. in order to arrive at the Feast of Booths and Tabernacles in 8 B.C.

A calculation going backwards from the Feast of Booths in 8 B.C. Julian may determine when the priests of the division of Abijah would have needed to have served in 9 B.C. Julian.

The Feast of Booths begins on Tishri 15 on the Jewish calendar. The Babylonian calendar lists Tishri 1 in 8 B.C., as 10/6 Julian. So, Tishri 15 would be 10/20, a Monday. Now, we can place the date 10/20, 8 B.C. Julian in the NASA date calculator and set the interval at minus 280 days.

That equals 40 weeks, the normal gestation period for a woman. It arrives at the date 1/13, 8 B.C. On the Jewish calendar that would be the last day of the month of Tebeth, unless the angel Gabriel came after sunset, then it would be the first day of Shebat. So, for sure, Jesus would have been conceived by Shebat 1.

Now, 1/13, 8 B.C. minus 177 days (29.5x6) is 7/20, 9 B.C., a Saturday, Ab 1 on the Jewish calendar. That is the date that John the Baptist would have been conceived in the womb of Elizabeth. It is good that it is a Saturday because each priestly division served one week at a time beginning on the afternoon of the first Sabbath until the forenoon of the following Sabbath.

Now, subtracting 7 days from 7/20, 9 B.C. arrives at 7/13, 9 B.C., a Saturday, and that is the beginning date that the division of Abijah would have needed to have served in the Temple.

Chart from first Sabbath course of Abijah serving in 9 B.C. to the beginning of the Feast of Booths on Tishri 15, 8 B.C.

9 B.C. Julian
Tammuz 23, Abijah 1st Sabbath
beginning afternoon, 7/13/9 B.C.
Ab 1, Abijah 2nd Sabbath forenoon
John conceived, 7/20/9 B.C.

Elul	1	6
Tishri	7	m
Heshvan	7	o
Kislev	d	n
Tebeth	a	t
8 B.C. Julian	ys	hs
Shebat 1, Jesus conceived		
Adar I	2	4	9
Adar II	8	0
Nisan	0	m
Lyyar	w	o
Sivan	d	e	n
Tammuz	a	e	t
Ab	y	k	h
Elul	s	s	s

Tishri 15 Jesus born on the 1st day of the Feast of Booths and Tabernacles

Israel museum model of the Temple before 70 A.D.
Photographed in Jerusalem by the author

In 70 A.D., the Roman Army killed the Jews inside the inner court area, including the priestly course of Jehoiarib that was serving at that time.

17

Feast of Booths and Tabernacles offerings that speak of the Messiah

The Israelites are to dwell in booths for seven days. The first day is a sacred assembly. Each day of the seven days they are to present an offering to the Lord made by fire. The eighth day is a closing sacred assembly. On the eighth day they are to present an offering to the Lord made by fire.

The Burnt-Offerings as they were preformed were foreshadows of aspects of the sacrificial atoning death of the Messiah, who is Jesus, on the cross that fulfilled all the offerings.

"There is no mention of sin in the Burnt-Offering. It speaks of Justification rather than forgiveness, and thus is a foreshadowing of the truth of Acts xiii:39, 'By Him all that believe are justified from all things.[1]'"

Through Justification the believer is pardoned, acquitted, and the righteousness of the Messiah is imputed to the believer. Imputed here means to have assigned a quality of value that one cannot attain on one's own. So, not only is the Feast of Booths a joyous celebration foreshadowing the birth of the Messiah; it also speaks of His righteousness.

1. The Study of Types, Ada R. Habershon (Kregel Publications Grand Rapids 1957) P. 87

Determining when the course of Abijah served

One source of information that facilitates a calculation is that the priestly course Jehoiarib was serving during the destruction of the Temple in 70 A.D.

Flavius Josephus, *A History of the Jewish Wars,* Book VI, Ch. IV, "But as for that house, God had for certain long ago doomed it to fire; and now that fatal day was come according to the revolution of ages: it was the tenth day of the month Lous [Roman] upon which it was formerly burnt by the king of Babylon."
"For the same month and day were now observed, as I said before, wherein the holy house was burnt formerly by the Babylonians."

Jeremiah 52:12-13 gives the fifth month, on the tenth *day* of the month [Ab 10] for the burning of the Temple, (which was the first Temple, the Temple originally built by Solomon).
Josephus says that the Jerusalem Temple was destroyed on Lous 10 (August 6, 70 A.D. Julian). However, he avoids saying it was the Romans that burnt it; rather he says that it was the same day that the ancient Babylonians destroyed Solomon's Temple (Ab 10, Hebrew).

Jewish tradition teaches that the Temple was destroyed on the day after the Sabbath, and that both Temples were destroyed on Ab 9. The one destroyed by the Romans on Ab 9 Jewish is August 5, 70 A.D. Julian.

Rabbi Yose ben Halafta (about 150 A.D.) is mentioned in the Jerusalem Talmud as saying that the course of Jehoiarib was serving in the Temple when it was destroyed by the Romans.

Therefore, the priestly course Jehoiarib began in the afternoon on the Sabbath of Ab 8 (August 4, 70 A.D.) and they were continuing their weekly service when the Temple was destroyed because both Ab 9 (Sunday) and Ab 10 (Monday) are in the week of the priestly service of Jehoiarib. It began in the afternoon Ab 8 and was supposed to continue until the forenoon of the following Sabbath, Ab 15.

The priestly course Jehoiarib was the first course in the order of the courses 1-24. Now, it has been determined that the priestly course Jehoiarib began serving on August 4, 70 A.D.

A calculation backward beginning with the course of Jehoiarib on Ab 8 (August 4, 70 A.D.); does indeed show that the priestly course Abijah did begin serving on July 13, 9 B.C.

Now, a calculation from August 4, 70 A.D. going backward to 9 B.C. and adjusting from the first course to the eighth course, that is the course of Abijah, arrives at July 13, 9 B.C. Lo and behold, July 13, 9 B.C. is the exact date the course of Abijah needed to begin on in order for Jesus to have been born during the Feast of Booths and Tabernacles in 8 B.C. Therefore, the chart shown earlier is correct to the exact day. The details of the actual calculation are shown later.

The priestly course of Abijah that Zachariah served in began on a Sabbath in the afternoon of Tammuz 23 (Hebrew), 7/13/9 B.C.

John was conceived on the following Sabbath in the forenoon of Ab 1 (Hebrew), 7/20/9 B.C. in the womb of Elizabeth.

177 days or 6 months later by 1/13/8 B.C., Shebat 1 (Hebrew), the first day of the month, Jesus was conceived in the womb of Mary.

Jesus was born 280 days, or 40 weeks, or 9 months later on Tishri 15 (Hebrew), the first day of the Feast of Booths and Tabernacles on October 20, 8 B.C.

Where Luke got the information concerning the birth of Jesus

In modern terms today, Luke would be called a journalist. He was an eyewitness to much of the ministry of the apostle Paul and he gathered information from other eyewitnesses too; then he recorded it in writing.

In Luke's writing, "The Acts of the Apostles," he describes that he was with Paul when they were traveling to Jerusalem. On the way there, Paul wrote II Corinthians. Titus left them to deliver II Corinthians to Corinth while Paul, Luke, and Timothy continued to Jerusalem.

On the way there they stayed many days at the home of Phillip the evangelist (Acts 21:8). As they were about to leave Phillip's home for Jerusalem, Luke says, **"We packed and went up to Jerusalem,"** (Acts 21:15).

The term **packed** indicates that they were bringing a lot of stuff with them as they traveled.

Luke had opportunity to speak face to face with the disciples of Jesus, who were eyewitnesses to Jesus.

And when we had come to Jerusalem, the brethren received us gladly. On the following *day* Paul went in with us to James, and all the elders were present, (Acts 21:17-18).

At Jerusalem, Paul spoke to James and the elders. Luke was there with them, for he uses the term **us**. Therefore, this confirms that Luke had face to face opportunities to gather information for the writing of his gospel. This time and many other times, for Luke affirms that he received information directly from eyewitnesses for the writing of his gospel.

Matt.13:55-56
55 "Is this not the carpenter's son? Is not His mother called Mary? And His brothers James, Joses, Simon, and Judas? 56 And His sisters, are they not all with us? Where then did this Man get all these things?"

Jesus had four brothers that are mentioned in the New Testament: James, Joses, Jude, and Simon. He also had two unnamed sisters or cousins. So, Luke had members of Jesus's own family available for sources of information. In addition, he had the gospel of Matthew.

Just as those who from the beginning were eyewitnesses and ministers of the word delivered them to us (Luke 1:2).

An uproar among the people developed in Jerusalem over Paul's position on the Jewish Law, especially in regards to Gentiles. He came under Roman protection and was bound by them at first, until he told them he was a Roman citizen. A hearing was held so the Romans could hear the charges against Paul, but nothing was settled. Eventually, Paul was escorted to Caesarea for his own safety. At first in Caesarea, even though Paul was in prison, he was not bound and allowed to have visitors. Luke would have been able to visit Paul in Prison.

So he commanded the centurion to keep Paul and to let *him* have liberty. And told him not to forbid any of his friends to provide for or visit him (Acts 24:23).

Paul was in Caesarea for at least two years. During those two years, Luke would have had opportunity to go back and forth between Caesarea and Jerusalem to interview the disciples of Jesus. He may have even met Mary the mother of Jesus, if she had lived past 75.

Luke clearly states that **a decree went out from Caesar Augustus that all the world should be registered**. In order to write that, Luke did not need to have known the exact date that Caesar Augustus gave that order; although, he might have known it. He only needed to write what was told to him. Likewise, Luke did not need to have known exactly when the division of Abijah served in the Temple when the angel appeared to Zachariah;

although, he might have known it. He only needed to write what was told to him. Luke 2:17 speaks of the shepherds that they made widely known the saying that was told to them concerning this child. (More details about the census in the end notes)

Continuing the chronology of Jesus in Matthew until the coming of the Magi 'wise men' and Jesus as a child

In Luke, the infancy narrative is written from the perspective of Mary, the mother of Jesus; whereas, in Matthew, the infancy narrative is written more from the perspective of Joseph.
Even though Matthew is the longest gospel of the three synoptic gospels, Mathew's infancy narrative features time compression and leaves out details that Luke fills in. Much of Matthew is devoted to demonstrating that Jesus is the fulfillment of many Old Testament scripture prophecies.

Matthew 1:18 After Mary is betrothed to Joseph, she is with child of the Holy Spirit. 1:19-21 Joseph is told in a dream that what is conceived in Mary is of the Holy Spirit, he should not be afraid to take Mary as his wife and to name his son Jesus, ('Yeshua' in Hebrew). 1:24-25 Then Joseph took Mary as his wife, and he did not know her until Jesus was born.

2:1 Now after Jesus was born in Bethlehem of Judea in the days of Herod the king, behold, magi from the east arrived in Jerusalem, 2:2 saying, "Where is He who has been born King of the Jews? For we have seen His star in the east and have come to worship Him." 2:3 When Herod the king heard this, he was troubled, and all Jerusalem with him. 2:4-5 Herod gathered the chief priests and the scribes together. He asked them, "Where is the Messiah to be born?" They told him in Bethlehem of Judea. 2:7 Herod secretly called the wise men to determine when the star first appeared. 2:8 Herod sent them to Bethlehem and told them to report back to him. 2:**9 When the wise men heard the King, they departed; and behold, the star which they had seen in the East went before them, until it came and stood over where the young child was.** 2:11 **And when they had come into the house, they saw the young child with Mary his mother, and fell down and worshiped Him.** 2:12 The wise men were warned in a dream not to return to Herod. 2:13 An angel appeared to Joseph in a dream telling him to take the young child and his mother, flee to Egypt until I bring you word. 2:16 Herod had the male children put to death in Bethlehem and districts around that area that were two years old and under according to the time he had learned from the wise men. 2:19-21 While Joseph was in Egypt, an angel appeared to him in a dream telling him to take the child and his mother to Israel for those who sought to kill the child are dead, then he arose and took them to Israel.

2:22-23 But when he heard Archelaus was reigning over Judea, he was afraid to go there. And being divinely warned by a dream, he turned aside into the parts of Galilee, and dwelt in the city of Nazareth, so that it might be fulfilled, which was spoken by the prophets, "He shall be called a Nazarene."

Following the far side of Judea along the coast of the Dead Sea and the Jordan river would lead to Galilee, which is beyond Judea and Samaria.

Commentary

Matt. 2:1 Now after Jesus was born in Bethlehem of Judea in the days of Herod the king. (At this point in the narrative there is a time gap.) The wise men came to Jerusalem at least a year after Jesus was born. Herold sent the wise men to Bethlehem, then the wisemen departed. The light, which was no ordinary light, reappeared at a critical time and led the wise men to the house where Jesus lived. Matthew does not make it clear exactly where the house was located; however, according to Luke, Jesus would have been in Nazareth at that time. After the wise men gave the family of Jesus valuable gifts, they left another way and did not return to Herod. Joseph was warned to take his family and flee to Egypt. Herod was king four more years after Jesus was born; hence, the danger of even staying.in Israel. Bethlehem is about six miles from Jerusalem. When the wise men did not report back to him, Herod sent men to kill all the boys in Bethlehem two years old and under.

Since it included two-year-old boys that indicates the wise men cane well after Jesus was born. The gifts the wise gave to Jesus helped Joseph, Mary and Jesus travel to Egypt and stay there a while. Years later, while Joseph, Mary, and Jesus are in Egypt, an angel appeared to Joseph in a dream telling him those who sought to kill the child are dead, go to Israel. Herod died in 4 B.C. So, Jesus would have been at least four years old, but he may have been older than that when they left Egypt.

Matthew and Luke do not contradict each other as some have claimed

Now, contrary to popular belief, Matthew does not mention the star as the star of Bethlehem, and does not say the star appeared after the wise men got to Bethlehem. Matt. 2:9 **When they heard the king, they departed; and behold, the star which they had seen in the East went before them, till it came and stood over where the young child was**. 2:11 **And when they had come into the house, they saw the young child with Marry His mother, and fell down and worshiped Him.**

That agrees with Luke, according to Luke by the time the wise men came at least a year after Jesus was born, He would have been home in Nazareth. The star was no ordinary star. In the Bible, there are many events in heaven concerning Jesus. Flavius Josephus mentions many events in heaven before the Romans attacked Jerusalem in 70 AD. Now, Matthrew does not say that Jesus lived in Bethlehem; he merely says that Jesus was born in Bethlehem, Luke describes how that came about. Defending the veracity of the scriptures is more important than defending our misguided beliefs.

Jesus as a young boy

Luke 2:41-48 Describes a time when Jesus was twelve years old. The family had gone to Jerusalem for the Passover. After a day's return journey, Joseph and Mary discovered that Jesus was not among the company returning home. They looked for Jesus for three days, then they found him in the Temple sitting with the teachers. All were astonished at his understanding. Mary said to Jesus that they had sought him anxiously.

2:49 **And He said to them, "Why did you seek Me? Did you not know that I must be about My Father's business?"**

2:51 Then Jesus went with them to Nazareth and was subject to them

John the Baptist

Luke begins the topic of John's ministry by dating when John began going around preaching repentance and baptizing people in the Jordan River.

Luke 3:1 **Now in the fifteenth year of the reign of Tiberius Caesar...** 3:2b **the word of the Lord came to John.**

John the Baptist began baptizing in the spring or summer of 29 A.D.

John prepared the way for Jesus with his baptism of repentance.

Luke mentions many groups of people that came to be baptized by John.

The topic of John baptizing certain groups of people continues until Jesus came to be baptized.

Luke 3:21 **"when all the people were baptized...Jesus was also baptized."**

After Jesus was baptized, it came to pass that the Holy Spirit alighted upon Jesus for the purpose of empowering him in his messianic mission.

The baptism of Jesus completes the topic of John's baptizing mission.

Jesus

Now in Luke 3:23, the topic changes to Jesus alone. The use of "Himself," as in "Jesus Himself," shows that a change in topic is intended.

Luke 3:23

Καὶ αὐτὸς ἦν ὁ Ἰησοῦς ὡσεὶ ἐτῶν
And Himself was Jesus about of years

τριάκοντα ἀρχόμενος ὢν
thirty beginning being

ὡς ἐνομίζετο
as *it* was supposed

And Jesus Himself *when* beginning was about thirty of years, being, as *it* was supposed.
(Author's translation)

The phrase, "as *it* was supposed," appears to refer to a source of information that Luke was using for dating Jesus. The most primary source for the early days of Jesus would have been His own brothers. There appears to be a hidden time gap between when Jesus set out on his own, according to Luke's source of information, and when He was baptized by John. That would explain Luke's use of indefinite terms.

Dating the birth of Jesus by using the date of the baptism of Jesus by John the Baptist

Luke 3:1 says that John was baptizing in the fifteenth year of Tiberius Caesar, which was 29 A.D.
Some have chosen to use the date of when John was baptizing to determine the date of the birth of Jesus.

Luke 3:23 And Jesus Himself *when* beginning was about thirty of years, being, as it is supposed. (author's translation).

In the first place, Luke is not claiming an exact date, as he uses the terms "about" and "it is supposed."

Secondly, it assumes that Jesus did not begin his ministry until he was baptized, which might, or might not, be true.

When Jesus was baptized, he physically took on the mission of the Messiah, 'the anointed one.'
After he came up out of the water and prayed, the Holy Spirit descended upon him.
Jesus may have devoted time in preparation for that role before He physically took on the mission of the Messiah at the time of His baptism.

The present-day popular date of 4 to 6 B.C. for the birth of Jesus

According to Josephus, Herod died after an eclipse of the moon. There was one that is dated March 13, 4 B.C. Also, Herod died only days after he had his son Antipater executed and before a Passover. The Passover on Nisan 15 in 4 B.C. was April 12.

The 4 B.C. date for the birth of Jesus uses the date that John began baptizing in 29 A.D. and the estimate that Jesus was about thirty years, "*when* beginning," while acknowledging that Herod died in 4 B.C.

At a minimum, the total would be: three years for 4 B.C. to 1 B.C., plus one year for 1 B.C. to 1 A.D., and 28 years for 1 A.D. to 29 A.D., for a total of 32 years.

In the first place, it is not meant to be an exact counting of years.
Furthermore, there is a question of what is meant by "*when* beginning."

This method gives priority to Luke's undefined estimate over Luke's specific statement of a census ordered by Caesar Augustus.

Dating based on Quirinius as Governor of Syria

The traditional English translation of Luke 2:2

Luke 2:2
2 **This census first took place while Quirinius was governing Syria**.

The traditional English translation of Luke 2:2 has led to unfair criticism of the veracity of Luke.
That is because both Luke and Matthew teach that Jesus was born while Herod was king of Israel. However, Herod died in 4 B.C., which was before Publius Sulpicius Quirinius (Cyrenius, Gk.) was governor of Syria 6 to 12 A.D. Therefore, Jesus could not have been born while Quirinius was governor of Syria, unless Quirinius was also governor before 4 B.C. However, the governors before 4 B.C. are known and Quirinius was not one of them. Critics have said things like, Luke was confused, and even that he just made it up. The problem with this translation is that it adds **while**, which is not in the Greek text, and that redates it to a time that is not what Luke intended to say; therefore, the difficulty many have had trying to interpret it. (See End Notes pp 51-55 for translation details)

Dating from "You are not yet fifty years old"

John 8:58 **Then the Jews said to him, "You are not yet fifty years old, and have you seen Abraham?"**

John was a disciple of Jesus; he is a primary source for this statement that he wrote. It should be given serious consideration.

The remark of the Jews spoken of in John 8:58 would have been after the second Passover in John 6:4. Since Jesus was crucified on April 3, 33 A.D., the remark of the Jews in John 8:58 would have been after the Passover of 32 A.D.

Therefore, given that Jesus was born in the fall of 8 B.C., which accounts for seven years going from 8 B.C. to 1 B.C., plus one year for 1 B.C. to 1 A.D., and 31 years to 32 A.D. Then Jesus would have been about 39 years old at the time the Jews made the remark, "You are not yet fifty."

Early Christian, Irenaeus Bishop of Lyons was of the opinion that Jesus was in His forties because to one thirty, they would have said that you are not yet forty. For they wanted to prove Him deceitful and would not have lengthened His age far beyond it. *Against Heresies* II. 22. 6

Calculating when the priestly course Abijah served
Information from Qumran Dead Sea Scrolls

Dr. John P. Platt (Astronomy Ph.D.) made a study of the Qumran Dead Sea Scrolls, especially 4Q320 and 4Q321, along with the Book of Enoch. John P. Pratt and his friend John C. Lefgren wrote an article that is in *Meridian Magazine* (12 Mar 2003). A reprint is available on the internet titled: Dead Sea Scrolls May Solve Mystery.

One method for calculating the courses of the priests is that each year the rotation begins in Nisan or Tishri and pauses during feast weeks when all the courses are need, then after the feast is over the rotation resumes. It has several problems.

Dr. Pratt speaks of Wed., 25 Mar., 42 B.C. to be an anchor date he has determined from the scrolls. Based on that date he calculated continuous cycles to the course of Jehoiarib in 70 A.D.

However, he does not show his calculations in the article. So, that is what we will need to do.

Unfortunately, John passed to the great beyond on October 12, 2021 due to COVID. I am thankful for his great work.

Ramifications of a continuous rotation

The main thing to be understood is that the priestly courses follow a continuous rotation. As a result of that each year happens to be 364 days. Therefore, even during the pilgrim feast days when all the priestly courses are needed, the rotation continues without a pause. After each course 1-24 has served, the rotation starts over and courses 1-24 serve again. Then two full rotations account for 48 weeks of each year and as the rotation continues, the courses advance four priestly courses in a 52-week year of 364-days each. In a 6-year cycle the Priestly courses advance four courses each year for six years for a total of 24 priestly courses. In a six-year cycle all the Priestly courses have been treated equally as to their time of service.

The priestly courses counting backward from the destruction of the Temple by the Romans in 70 A.D. Julian

Ab 10 Jewish, Josephus's date for destruction of the Temple, which is 8/6, 70 A.D.
Ab 9 Jewish, a day after the Sabbath, the date Jews use, which is Sunday, 8/5, 70 A.D.
Course 1. Jehoiarib, began at noon on the Sabbath of Ab 8, which is 8/4, 70 A.D., and was still serving when the Temple was destroyed.

Calculating interval of courses backwards

The priestly courses 1. through 24., each began serving in the afternoon of a certain Sabbath (Saturday) and continued serving the weekly service until the forenoon of the following Sabbath.

All calculations begin with course 1. Jehoiarib that began serving on the Sabbath in the afternoon of Ab 8 (8/4, 70 A.D.) and continued serving the weekly service until the Temple was destroyed. The following calculates from 8/4, 70 A.D. going backward to previous courses that served before the Temple was destroyed. The 1st Sabbath was in the afternoon and the 2nd Sabbath in the forenoon.

Course number -days afternoon to forenoon

1. Jehoiarib (8/4) Aug. 4, 1st Sabbath afternoon, 70 A.D.

24. Maaziah (8/4 -7 days) Jul. 28 to Aug. 4, 70 A.D

23. Delaiah (8/4 -14 days) Jul. 21 to Jul. 28, 70 A.D.

22. Gamul   (8/4 -21 days) Jul. 14 to Jul. 21, 70 A.D.

21. Jachin   (8/4 -28 days) Jul. 7 to Jul. 14, 70 A.D.

20. Jehezekel (8/4 -35 days) Jun. 30 to Jul. 7, 70 A.D.

19. Pethahiah (8/4 -42 days) Jun. 23 to Jun. 30, 70 A.D.

18. Happizzez (8/4 -49 days) Jun. 16 to Jun. 23, 70 A.D.

17. Hezir   (8/4 -56 days) Jun. 9 to Jun. 16, 70 A.D.

16. Immer   (8/4 -63 days) Jun. 2 to Jun. 9, 70 A.D.

15. Bilgah   (8/4 -70 days) May 26 to Jun. 2, 70 A.D.

14. Jeshebeab (8/4 -77 days) May 19 to May 26, 70 A.D.

13. Huppah   (8/4 -84 days) May 12 to May 19, 70 A.D.

12. Jakim   (8/4 -91 days) May 5 to May 12, 70 A.D.

11. Eliashib (8/4 -98 days) Apr. 28 to May 5, 70 A.D.

10. Shecaniah (8/4 -105 days) Apr. 21 to Apr. 28, 70 A.D.

9. Jeshua   (8/4 -112 days) Apr. 14 to Apr. 21, 70 A.D.

8. Abijah   (8/4 -119 days) Apr. 7 to Apr. 14, 70 A.D.

7. Hakkoz   (8/4 -126 days) Mar. 31 to Apr. 7, 70 A.D.

6. Mijamin (8/4 -133 days) Mar. 24 to Mar. 31, 70 A.D.

5. Malchijah (8/4 -140 days) Mar. 17 to Mar. 24, 70 A.D.

4. Seorim   (8/4 -147 days) Mar. 10 to Mar. 17, 70 A.D.

3. Harim   (8/4 -154 days) Mar. 3 to Mar. 10, 70 A.D.

2. Jedaiah   (8/4 -161 days) Feb. 24 to Mar. 3, 70 A.D.

1. Jehoiarib (8/4 -168 days) Feb. 17 to Feb. 24, 70 A.D.

So, after 168 days, the cycle is complete. The 24 priestly courses each serve one week continuously and complete a cycle every 7 x 24 equals 168 days.

Calculating Priestly courses backward from August 4, 70 A.D. in 6-year cycles.

Now, a 6-year repeating cycle of 52 weeks per 364-day year equals 312 weeks, then 312 weeks times 7 days per week equals 2184-days per 6-year cycle. Now, a 2184-day cycle that begins on a Sabbath will arrive on another Sabbath. The website: Julian Day Number Calculations — NASA, works well for this because the Julian day astronomers use begins at noon and goes until noon the following day, the same way that the Jewish priestly weekly service starts at noon on a Sabbath and goes until noon the following Sabbath. The negative numbers are numbers that are entered into a Julian date calculator for a Julian date that many days earlier.

The 6-year cycle 1
Aug. 4, 70 A.D. -2184 days equals Aug. 11, 64 A.D.

The 6-year cycle 2
Aug. 4, 70 A.D. -4368 days equals Aug. 19, 58 A.D.

The 6-year cycle 3
Aug. 4, 70 A.D. -6552 days equals Aug. 26, 52 A.D.

The 6-year cycle 4
Aug. 4, 70 A.D. -8736 days equals Sep. 3, 46 A.D.

The 6-year cycle 5
Aug. 4, 70 A.D. -10920 days equals Sep 10, 40 A.D.

The 6-year cycle 6
Aug. 4, 70 A.D. -13104 days equals Sep. 18, 34 A.D.

The 6-year cycle 7
Aug. 4, 70 A.D. -15288 days equals Sep 25, 28 A.D.

The 6-year cycle 8
Aug. 4, 70 A.D. -17472 days equals Oct. 3, 22 A.D.

The 6-year cycle 9
Aug. 4, 70 A.D. -19656 days equals Oct. 10, 16 A.D.

The 6-year cycle 10
Aug. 4, 70 A.D. -21840 days equals Oct. 18, 10 A.D.

The 6-year cycle 11
Aug. 4, 70 A.D. -24024 days equals Oct. 25, 4 A.D.

NASA calculator adjusted correctly going 1 A.D. to B.C. 1 because the Julian calendar has no zero and counts 1. twice.

The 6-year cycle 12
Aug. 4, 70 A.D. −26208 days equals Nov. 2, 3 B.C.

The 6-year cycle 13
Aug. 4, 70 A.D. -28392 days equals Nov. 9, 9 B.C.

For converting from course 1. Jehoiarib to course 8. Abijah going backwards, then 119 more days need to be subtracted. Actually, the calculation is based on number of days according to the priestly cycle. The Julian date is only a way of defining it.

Aug. 4, 70 A.D. -28511 days equals Jul 13, 9 B.C.

July 13, 9 B.C. is the exact day that the priestly course Abijah needed to have begun according to the chart for Jesus to have been born on the first day of the Feast of Booths in 8 B.C.

Julian Day Number Calculations —NASA

Julian Day and Civil Day Calculator

Aug ∨ 4 ∨ 70 A.D. ∨ is a Saturday
whose Julian Day Number is 1746841
Calendar: ○ Auto (Julian/Gregorian) ◉ Julian Only

(Edit the following field for interval calculations.)
is followed -28511 days later by

Jul ∨ 13 ∨ 9 B.C. ∨ is a Saturday
whose Julian Day Number is 1718330
Calendar: ○ Auto (Julian/Gregorian) ◉ Julian Only

1. You must have JavaScript enabled in your browser for this calculator to work. Requires Netscape 3.0 or Internet Explorer 3.0 or later for correct operation.
2. All fields are editable. Change civil date to calculate Julian Day Number and day-of-week, or vice versa.
3. After changing a text box, click outside of the calculator, or press tab, to update all other data. (Don't press return.)
4. In Auto mode, civil calendar changes from Julian to Gregorian between October 5/16, 1582. For Julian civil dates after that date, as in England and colonies until 1753, select Julian Only.

Jul ∨ 13 ∨ 9 B.C. ∨ is a Saturday
whose Julian Day Number is 1718330
Calendar: ○ Auto (Julian/Gregorian) ◉ Julian Only

(Edit the following field for interval calculations.)
is followed 7 days later by

Jul ∨ 20 ∨ 9 B.C. ∨ is a Saturday
whose Julian Day Number is 1718337
Calendar: ○ Auto (Julian/Gregorian) ◉ Julian Only

1. You must have JavaScript enabled in your browser for this calculator to work. Requires Netscape 3.0 or Internet Explorer 3.0 or later for correct operation.
2. All fields are editable. Change civil date to calculate Julian Day Number and day-of-week, or vice versa.
3. After changing a text box, click outside of the calculator, or press tab, to update all other data. (Don't press return.)
4. In Auto mode, civil calendar changes from Julian to Gregorian between October 5/16, 1582. For Julian civil dates after that date, as in England and colonies until 1753, select Julian Only.

Jul ∨ 20 ∨ 9 B.C. ∨ is a Saturday
whose Julian Day Number is 1718337
Calendar: ○ Auto (Julian/Gregorian) ◉ Julian Only

(Edit the following field for interval calculations.)
is followed 177 days later by

Jan ∨ 13 ∨ 8 B.C. ∨ is a Monday
whose Julian Day Number is 1718514
Calendar: ○ Auto (Julian/Gregorian) ◉ Julian Only

1. You must have JavaScript enabled in your browser for this calculator to work. Requires Netscape 3.0 or Internet Explorer 3.0 or later for correct operation.
2. All fields are editable. Change civil date to calculate Julian Day Number and day-of-week, or vice versa.
3. After changing a text box, click outside of the calculator, or press tab, to update all other data. (Don't press return.)
4. In Auto mode, civil calendar changes from Julian to Gregorian between October 5/16, 1582. For Julian civil dates after that date, as in England and colonies until 1753, select Julian Only.

Jan ∨ 13 ∨ 8 B.C. ∨ is a Monday
whose Julian Day Number is 1718514
Calendar: ○ Auto (Julian/Gregorian) ◉ Julian Only

(Edit the following field for interval calculations.)
is followed 280 days later by

Oct ∨ 20 ∨ 8 B.C. ∨ is a Monday
whose Julian Day Number is 1718794
Calendar: ○ Auto (Julian/Gregorian) ◉ Julian Only

1. You must have JavaScript enabled in your browser for this calculator to work. Requires Netscape 3.0 or Internet Explorer 3.0 or later for correct operation.
2. All fields are editable. Change civil date to calculate Julian Day Number and day-of-week, or vice versa.
3. After changing a text box, click outside of the calculator, or press tab, to update all other data. (Don't press return.)
4. In Auto mode, civil calendar changes from Julian to Gregorian between October 5/16, 1582. For Julian civil dates after that date, as in England and colonies until 1753, select Julian Only.

A calculation of the 168-day intervals when the course of Abijah served in the Temple from 9 B.C. until 4 B.C. demonstrates that July 13, 9 B.C. is the only date that arrives at the time of the Feast of Booths.

1st Sabbath	2nd Sabbath	+177 days	+280 days
Of Abijah	John conceived	Jesus conceived	Jesus born

8/4/70 A.D. -28511 days for 8. Abijah
7/13/9 B.C. 7/20/9 B.C. 1/13/8 B.C. 10/20/8 B.C.
Tammuz 23 Ab 1   Shebat 1   Tishri 15

-28392 -119 = -28511 days for 8. Abijah
The 6-year cycle 13, -28392 days for 1. Jehoiarib
-28392 +49 = -28343 days for 8. Abijah

1st Sabbath 2nd Sabbath +177 days +280 days

+168 days earlier
8/4/70 A.D. -28343 days for 8. Abijah
12/28/9 B.C. 1/4/8 B.C.   6/30/8 B.C. 4/6/7 B.C.
                                                            Nisan 5

+168 days earlier
8/4/70 A.D. -28175 days for 8. Abijah
6/14/8 B.C. 6/21/8 B.C. 12/15/8 B.C. 9/21/7 B.C.
                                                            Elul 26

45

1st Sabbath 2nd Sabbath +177 days +280 days

+168 days earlier
8/4/70 A.D. -28007 days for 8 Abijah
11/29/8 B.C. 12/6/8 B.C. 6/1/7 B.C.   3/8/6 B.C.
                                                    Adar 17

+168 days earlier
8/4/70 A.D. -27839 days for 8. Abijah
5/16/7 B.C. 5/23/7 B.C. 11/16/7 B.C. 8/23/6 B.C.
                                                    Ab 7

+168 days earlier
8/4/70 A.D. -27671 days for 8. Abijah
10/31/7 B.C. 11/7/7 B.C. 5/3/6 B.C.   2/7/5 B.C.
                                                    Tebeth 28

+168 days earlier
8/4/70 A.D. -27503 days for 8. Abijah
4/17/6 B.C. 4/24/6 B.C. 10/18/6 B.C. 7/24/5 B.C.
                                                    Tammuz 19

+168 days earlier
8/4/70 A.D. -27335 days for 8. Abijah
10/2/6 B.C. 10/9/6 B.C. 4/3/5 B.C.   1/8/4 B.C.
                                                    Tebeth 9

Herod king of Israel died between 3/13 and a
Passover, which in 4 B.C. was 4/12/4 B.C.

1st Sabbath 2nd Sabbath +177 days +280 days

+168 days earlier
8/4/70 A.D. -27167 days for 8. Abijah
3/18/5 B.C. 3/25/5 B.C. 9/18/5 B.C. 6/25/4 B.C.
                                    Tammuz 1

+168 days earlier
8/4/70 A.D. -26999 days for 8. Abijah
9/2/5 B.C. 9/9/5 B.C. 3/5/4 B.C. 12/10/4 B.C.
                                    Kislev 20

+168 days earlier
8/4/70 A.D. -26831 days for 8. Abijah
2/17/4 B.C. 2/24/4 B.C. 8/20/4 B.C. 5/27/3 B.C.
                                    Lyyar 12

+168 days earlier
8/4/70 A.D. -26663 days for 8. Abijah
8/4/4 B.C. 8/11/4 B.C. 2/4/3 B.C. 11/11/3 B.C.
                                    Heshvan 1

+168 days earlier
8/4/70 A.D. -26495 days for 8. Abijah
1/19/3 B.C. 1/26/3 B.C. 7/22/3 B.C. 4/28/2 B.C.
                                    Nisan 23

1st Sabbath 2nd Sabbath +177 days +280 days

+168 days earlier
8/4/70 A.D. -26327 days for 8. Abijah
7/6/3 B.C.   7/13/3 B.C.   1/6/2 B.C.   10/13/2 B.C.
                                                    Tishri 13

-26208 -119 = -26327 days for 8 Abijah
The 6-year cycle 12, -26208 days for 1. Jehoiarib
-26208 +49 = -26159 days for 8 Abijah

+168 days earlier
8/4/70 A.D. -26159 days for 8. Abijah
12/21/3 B.C. 12/28/3 B.C. 6/23/2 B.C. 3/29/1 B.C.
                                                    Nisan 4

+168 days earlier
8/4/70 A.D. -25991 days for 8. Abijah
6/7/2 B.C.   6/14/2 B.C.   12/8/2 B.C.   9/13/1 B.C.
                                                    Elul 25

It is interesting that from when Jesus was born on October 20, 8 B.C. to when Jesus was crucified on April 3, 33 A.D. is a span of 14410 days.
Now, 14410 days is 39.45 years Julian; however, 14410 days divided by a 360-day year equals a span of 40 years. The number 40 is a number that occurs quite often in the Bible scriptures.
A 360-day year is the prophetic year used in Daniel and Revelation.

End Notes

Roman Census

Over a period of many years there were many Roman censuses taken.
86/85 B.C. 463,000
70/69 B.C. 910,000/900,000
28 B.C. (Augustus) 4,063,000
8 B.C. (Augustus) 4,233,000
A.D. 14. (Augustus) 4,937,000

The Augustus censuses are several times greater than previous censuses. That indicates either a much larger territory was being counted, and/or, a change in the rules concerning who should be counted.

Source of the count is the website: Roman Census Figures – California State University Northridge. The author is John Paul Adams.

Sources are:
*Arnold J. Toynbee, *Hannibal's Legacy* (Oxford 1965) Volume I, Chapter III Annex 10.
*Tenney Frank, "Roman Census Statistics from 508 to 225 B.C., "American Journal of Philology 51 (1930) 313-324

Critics say that there is no proof the census included more than Romans and they say that if it had happened to include Israel, there would have been a demonstration.

Both Luke and Matthew affirm that Jesus was born during the time when Herod was king of Israel. Herod was subject to the Roman Empire. So, there was a reason to include Israel. It was only a census, and it was during Herod's reign. Herod was a cruel king; he was not a Roman outsider. So, it is not fair to compare it with later times after Herod's death.

Luke says that he got it from eyewitnesses. As I wrote before, Jesus had four brothers mentioned in the New Testament. Luke could have easily had face to face contact with the brothers of Jesus when he went to Jerusalem with Paul; he did not get his information from some Roman archive. Luke was closer to the actual time of when it happened than Josephus or other writers that modernists follow. Those arguments from silence do not stand up against Luke's accurate dating account.

The only census during that time of the dimension that Luke describes in Luke 2:1, **"That all the world should be registered"** is the 8 B.C. census.

The Grammar of Luke 2:2

Quirinius was well known in Judaea due to the census he carried out that included Judaea after he became governor of Syria in 6 A.D. Many have said that Acts 5:37 refers to that census, so in that case, Luke was fully aware of that census. Since Quirinius was a well-known person throughout the Roman Empire, Luke uses Quirinius as a reference point to date the census of Caesar Augustus as former of Quirinius, the one we date as in 8 B.C. Now, Luke 2:2 does not make a direct reference to the census by Quirinius, but some translations tend to involve it in some way.

As a comparison of order between two.

Luke 2:2

Αὕτη	ἡ	ἀπογραφὴ	πρώτη	ἐγένετο
This	the	registration	former	*it* was
			earlier	

ἡγεμονεύοντος	τῆς	Συρίας	Κυρηνίου
of governing	of the	of Syria	of Quirinius

Where ἀπογραφὴ a feminine noun followed by the feminine πρώτη acting as an adjective is translated by the adjective **former**.

For manuscripts with or without ἡ, see: New Testament Greek Manuscripts Luke, Ed. Reuben Swanson (William Carey International University Press; Pasadena, CA) 30

51

The Greek word ἀπογραφη 'registration' is a feminine noun in the nominative case, making it the subject of the sentence. It refers back to ἀπογράφεσθαι 'to be registered' in Luke 2:1. πρώτη is a nominative singular feminine form of πρῶτος.

The sentence ends with a genitive absolute that acts as a unit.

The comparison between two that is meant is between the registration and the genitive absolute.

Walter Bauer is among the best Greek scholars of modern time and according to him: πρῶτος *first* of several, but also when only two persons or things are involved (= πρότερος).[1]

Then under πρότερος comp. of πρό 1.a. *former, earlier.*[2]

πρό a preposition with a genitive, *before.*

The Zondervan NIV Bible Commentary acknowledges it can be translated as "former" or "prior."

2. The word translated "first" can also mean "former" or "prior." This makes the meaning of v.2. "This census was *before* that made when Quirinius was governor."[3]

By the use of **former** in Luke 2:2, Luke is clarifying that it was not the census carried out by Quirinius because it was former of Quirinius governing Syria. He is using Quirinius as a way of dating the registration that was ordered by Caesar Augustus as earlier then Quirinius governing Syria.

Then, as a comparison of order between two, the literal translation is as follows:
This registration was former of Quirinius governing Syria.

This translation does not add or subtract any words to or from the Greek text.
Whether Luke uses governing, or governor, is immaterial because it was former of Quirinius.

1. A Greek-English Lexicon of the New Testament and Other Early Christian Literature. Walter Bauer Trans. By William F. Arndt and F. Wilbur Gingrich; (The University of Chicago Press; Limited Edition licensed to Zondervan Publishing House 1952) p.732

2. IBID., p. 729

3. Zondervan NIV Bible Commentary Vol. 2 New Testament; Kenneth L. Barker & John R. Kohlenberger III; Zondervan 1994) p. 217

English Traditional Translation

The English translation of Luke 2:2 for many years in the popular Bible versions is as follows:

Luke 2:2
2 This census first took place while Quirinius was governing Syria.

Αὕτη ἡ ἀπογραφὴ πρώτη
This the census first *took place*

ἐγένετο ἡγεμονεύοντος
he was *while* of governing

τῆς Συρίας **Κυρηνίου**
of the of Syria of Quirinius

The traditional English translation of Luke 2:2 has led to unfair criticism of the veracity of Luke. That is because both Luke and Matthew teach that Jesus was born while Herod was king of Israel. However, Herod died in 4 B.C., which was before Publius Sulpicius Quirinius was governor of Syria from 6 to 12 A.D. Therefore, Jesus could not have been born while Quirinius was governor of Syria, unless Quirinius was also governor before 4 B.C. However, the governors are: "9 - 7/6 B.C. Gaius Sentius Saturninus, 7/6 - 4 B.C. Publius Quinctilius Varus, 4 B.C. - 1 A.D. Unkown."
List of Roman governors of Syria 27 B.C.-135 A.D. Wikipedia

The 4 B.C.-1 A.D. Unknown Governor
There is an inscription speaking of someone being governor of Syria twice, but the name is missing. Apparently, during much of this time Quirinius was still leading battles against certain tribes. Furthermore, that date would require redating the death of Herod and proving that there was a census ordered by Augustus at that time, a difficult task.

The traditional English translation does not clarify what Luke said in verse 2:1. Rather by adding the word **while**, it redates the time of the census to a time Luke did not intend to say.

Some have suggested that it could be translated adverbially as "This census was before Quirinius governing Syria." The objection to translating it adverbially as "before" is that there is a verb in between πρώτη and the genitive absolute. On the other hand, the verb may be there to make it even more clear that a comparison of order between two is intended. "Former" is the correct translation of the πρώτη when there is a comparison of only two, which is the case in Luke 2:2.

Conclusion

It is required that the Feast of Tabernacles and Booths refers to the Messiah.

Answer one:
The residents making Burnt-Offerings to the Lord is a foreshowing of justification by means of the righteousness of the Messiah imputed to believers. It is required that it refers to Jesus because Burnt-Offerings speak of Justification. Justification is not possible apart from the imputed righteousness of the Messiah.
The residents are to dwell in booths for seven days and each day of the seven-days, they are to make offerings with fire to the Lord.
Hebrews 10:4 **For it is not possible that the blood of bulls and goats could take away sins**. If the blood of bulls and goats cannot take away sins, then for sure, they cannot impart righteousness. When offerings and sacrifices were made, God looked forward to the life and atoning sacrificial death of Jesus on the cross.
Jesus fulfilled all the offerings and sacrifices, even the grain offerings.

Answer two:
The residents making Burnt-Offerings to the Lord without intervening priests is a foreshadowing of the priesthood of the believer in the Messiah.

It is required that it refers to the Messiah, Jesus, because the very residents dwelling in the booths are themselves to make offerings to the Lord without the need for an intervening priest. That speaks of another aspect of the work of the Messiah, Jesus. Psalm 110 is a Messianic Psalm of David. Psalm 110:4 **The Lord has sworn and will not relent, "You are a priest forever according to the order of Melchizedek."** Hebrews applies this verse to Jesus in 5:10, 7:17, and 7:21. Jesus is a High Priest as sworn by the Lord. Directly to him we can go, for Jesus makes the believer a priest over his or her own soul.

Jesus Christ is the high priest; He makes those in Christ a priest over their own soul.

Revelation 1:6
6 **And made us a kingdom, priests to His God and Father — to Him *be* the glory and dominion forever and ever. Amen.**
Holman Christian Standard Bible (Nashville: Holman Bible Publishers, 2003)

6 καὶ ἐποίησε ἡμᾶς βασιλείαν ἱερεῖς
  And He made us   a kingdom   priests

τῷ θεῷ καὶ Πατρὶ αὐτοῦ
to God and Father of him

57

At the present time Christians are a Kingdom of Priests. Jesus made each Christian believer within the Kingdom of God a priest over his or her own soul. βασιλείαν ἱερεῖς **'a kingdom priests'** are nouns in apposition in the accusative case, in other words the direct object case. A noun is in apposition when added to another noun of the same case to explain it or define it. In the same way **priests** defines **a kingdom**; then everyone in the kingdom is a priest unto one's own self. Furthermore, the **He** in **He made us a kingdom, priests to His God and Father** refers to Jesus Christ in Rev. 1:5. Jesus Christ has made each Christian believer a priest over her or his own soul.

* The pronoun **us** is omitted in the United Bible Societies *The Greek New Testament*. It appears in א (Sinaiticus manuscript) τῷ θεῷ ἡμᾶς 'to the God of us'
37. *The NKJV Greek English Interlinear New Testament* (Nashville: Thomas Nelson Publishers, 1994), xviii.

Answer three:
The birth of the Messiah should be a joyous celebration and it is.
The residents of the Feast of Booths are to be joyful. The angel said to the shepherds, **"I bring you good tidings of great joy, which will be to all people."**

Answer four:

It demonstrates that God is true to His word.

The Feast of Booths is a celebration foreshadowing the birth of the Messiah. Jesus was born during the Feast of Booths because God is true to His word.

It is very important to demonstrate that the Feasts commanded by God relate to the Messiah.

When God told Moses concerning the celebration of the Feast of Booths and Tabernacles, the day of the month, and the Burnt-Offering requirements, God had foreknowledge of when and how the Messiah would be born. The accuracy of the calculation demonstrates that.

Answer five:

It upholds the veracity of Luke.

The exact calculation upholds the veracity of Luke on the matter. Critics have said various things from Luke was mixed up to Luke made it up. All because Luke 2:2 was translated to say what Luke did not intend to say.

Answer six:

The Feast of Trumpets as described in Lev. 23:23-25, foreshadows an event still in the future.

It is important to demonstrate that all the Feasts that were commanded by God relate to the Messiah, and or, the Holy Spirit. That is because the Feast of Trumpets foreshadows an event still in the future.

It is crucial that all the people of the world understand the significance of the Feast of Trumpets. It consists of blowing trumpets for one day. It foreshadows I Thessalonians 4:16-17.

4:16 **For the Lord Himself will descend from heaven with a shout, with the voice of an archangel, and with the trumpet of God. And the dead in Christ will rise first. 17 Then we who are alive *and* remain shall be caught up together with them in the clouds to meet the Lord in the air. And thus we shall always be with the Lord.**

This passage describes the second coming of the Lord Jesus in the air to gather His assembly, those in Christ, including Old Testament saints.

Christmas

The Feast of Booths is a time of joyous celebration for the Jews that relates to the exodus out of Egypt and the gathering of the harvest.

Christians should not at this time change the time of celebrating Christmas to the time of the Feast of Booths. Jesus fulfilled the Feast of Booths, just as, He fulfilled the Passover. That is why the Apostle Paul is quoted in Acts as saying that he wants to go to Jerusalem for Pentecost. Paul does not say that he wants to go to Jerusalem for the Passover because Jesus is our Pesach, Lamb.

Christians should just be aware that Jesus was born during the Feast of Booths and Tabernacles.

How to become a Christian

To become a Christian—one must repent, believe, and receive.

One becomes born again by repenting of one's own sins and exercising faith in the Lord Jesus Christ as one's own Lord and savior.

Ephesians 2:8-9
8 **For by grace you have been saved through faith, and that not of yourselves;** *it is* **the gift of God,** 9 **not of works, lest anyone should boast.**

1 John 1:9
9 **If we confess our sins, He is faithful and just to forgive us** *our* **sins and to cleanse us from all unrighteousness.**

Romans 10:9-10
9 **That if you confess with your mouth the Lord Jesus and believe in your heart that God has raised Him from the dead, you will be saved.** 10 **For with the heart one believes unto righteousness, and with the mouth confession is made unto salvation.**

Commentary

A popular conception of faith is that faith is a belief in something without proof. That is not Christian faith! Christian faith is something, or someone you put your trust in and live by! Living by faith is a commitment!

We are not saved by works we have done; we are saved by what Christ has done for us. According to the saying, "Not saved by good works, saved unto good works."

A prayer to become a Christian.

Walk the path of Faith

Acknowledge it is true
"I believe"

I acknowledge that I am a sinner. I believe Jesus is the Lord. I believe Jesus is the Messiah, (the Christ). I believe that Jesus (who is the Christ) died on the cross and paid the penalty for sinners. I believe that Jesus rose again from the grave and lives forever more.

Receive it for yourself
"For me"

My God and Heavenly Father, I repent of all my sins. Forgive me of my sins because Jesus paid the penalty for my sins when He died on the cross for me.

Lord Jesus, be my Lord and my savior, and forgive me of my sins and cleanse me from all unrighteousness. Make me a new creation in Christ by the power of the Holy Spirit. Jesus, be my mediator before God now and on judgment day, and make me priest over my own soul.

Claim it as fulfilled and live accordingly
"Thank you, Lord"

Jesus, thank you for dying on the cross for me and help me to live for you now and forever. In Jesus name I pray, amen!

Direct Quotes

Gen. 33:17, p. 4	1:36-37, p. 12	John 8:58, p. 35
Lev. 23:33-44, p, 5-6	2:1, p. 3	Acts 21:15, p. 22
Psalm 110:4, p. 59	2:2, p. 3,34, 53,54	21:17-18, p. 22
Matt. 2:9,11, p. 26,28	2:3-7, p. 6	24:23, p. 24
13:55-56, p. 23	2:21 p. 8	Rom. 10:9-10, p, 61
Luke 1:2, p. 23	2:22-24, p. 9	Eph. 2:8-9, p. 61
1:5-14, p. 10	2:39, p. 9	I Thess. 4:16-17, p. 60
1:26-27, p. 12	2:49, p. 29	Heb. 10;4, p. 56
1:30-31, p. 12	3:21, p. 30	I John 1:9, p. 61
		Rev. 1:6, p. 57

Babylonian Calendar 9 B.C. to 1 B.C.

B.C.	Nisanu	Aiaru	Simanu	Duzu	Abu	Ululu	Ululu II	Tashritu	Arahsamnu	Kislimu	B.C.	Tebetu	B.C.	Shabatu	Addaru	Addaru II
9	3/25	4/23	5/23	6/21	7/20	8/18	9/17	10/17	11/15	12/15	8	1/14		2/12	3/14	
8	4/13	5/12	6/10	7/10	8/8	9/7		10/6	11/4	12/4	7	1/3		2/1	3/3	
7	4/2	5/1	5/31	6/29	7/29	8/27		9/26	10/25	11/24		12/23	6	1/22	2/20	3/22
6	4/20	5/20	6/19	7/18	8/17	9/15		10/15	11/14	12/13	5	1/11		2/10	3/10	
5	4/8	5/8	6/7	7/6	8/5	9/4		10/4	11/2	12/2		12/31	4	1/29	2/27	
4	3/29	4/27	5/27	6/25	7/25	8/24		9/23	10/23	11/21		12/21	3	1/19	2/17	3/18
3	4/17	5/16	6/15	7/14	8/13	9/12		10/12	11/11	12/10	2	1/8		2/7	3/8	
2	4/6	5/6	6/4	7/4	8/2	9/1		10/1	10/31	11/29		12/29	1	1/27	2/26	

64

B.C.	Nisan	Iyyar	Sivan	Tammuz	Ab	Elul	Tishri	Heshvan	Kislev	B.C.	Tebeth	B.C.	Shebat	Adar	Adar II
9	3/25	4/23	5/23	6/21	7/20	8/18	9/17	10/17	11/15		12/15	8	1/14	2/12	3/14
8	4/13	5/12	6/10	7/10	8/8	9/7	10/6	11/4	12/4	7	1/3		2/1	3/3	
7	4/2	5/1	5/31	6/29	7/29	8/27	9/26	10/25	11/24		12/23	6	1/22	2/20	3/22
6	4/20	5/20	6/19	7/18	8/17	9/15	10/15	11/14	12/13	5	1/11		2/10	3/10	
5	4/8	5/8	6/7	7/6	8/5	9/4	10/4	11/2	12/2		12/31	4	1/29	2/27	
4	3/29	4/27	5/27	6/25	7/25	8/24	9/23	10/23	11/21		12/21	3	1/19	2/17	3/18
3	4/17	5/16	6/15	7/14	8/13	9/12	10/12	11/11	12/10	2	1/8		2/7	3/8	
2	4/6	5/6	6/4	7/4	8/2	9/1	10/1	10/31	11/29		12/29	1	1/27	2/26	

Hebrew Calendar 9 B.C. to 1 B.C.
Hebrew calendar cannot have an intercalary month between Nisan and Tishri

65

Babylonian calendar, 445–444 B.C. when Artaxerxes was king of Persia

Artaxerxes	Nisanu	Aiaru	Simanu	Duzu	Abu	Ululu	Ululu II	Tashritu	Arahsamnu	Kislimu	B.C.	Tebetu	B.C.	Shabatu	Addaru	Addaru II
20 445	4/13	5/12	6/11	7/11	8/9	9/8		10/8	11/6	12/6	**444**	1/4		2/3	3/4	
21 444	4/3	5/2	6/1	6/30	7/30	8/28	9/27	10/26	11/25		443	12/25		1/23	2/22	3/23

Babylonian Chronology 626 B.C.–A.D. 75 by R. A. Parker and W. H. Dubberstein; Wipf & Stock, p. 32

The Babylonians used the first month for counting the year of the king. The Babylonian captives from Judah used the Babylonian calendar, but continued to use Nisan, the first month, for the beginning of ecclesiastical year and Tishri, the seventh month, for counting the year of the king.

66

Hebrew Calendar showing the date of twentieth year of Artaxerxes.

Artaxerxes	B.C.	Nisan	Iyyar	Sivan	Tammuz	Ab	Elul	Tishri	Heshvan	Kislev	B.C.	Tebeth	B.C.	Shebat	Adar	Adar II
19	445	4/13	5/12	6/11	7/11	8/9	9/8	10/8	11/6	12/6	444	1/4			2/3	3/4
20	444	4/3	5/2	6/1	6/30	7/30	8/28	9/27	10/26	11/25		12/25	443	1/23	2/22	3/23

Nehemiah received letters to rebuild the wall of Jerusalem on Nisan, in the twentieth year of Artaxerxes. The Babylonian captives from Judah counted the year of the king beginning with seventh month, after he became king. The twentieth year of Artaxerxes was 444 B.C., and that year, Nisan began on April 3.

Read, *The Seventy Sevens Prophecy told to Daniel by the Angel Gabriel* for calculating the seven sevens and sixty-two sevens until the coming of the Messiah.

67

The Seventy Sevens Prophecy Told to Daniel by The Angel Gabriel, By Douglas Wayne Ophus

The first book that correctly calculates the seven sevens and sixty-two sevens until the coming of the Messiah to the day of the Triumphal Entry of Jesus into Jerusalem.

Book back cover picture in grayscale

FUTURE HISTORY BEFORE IT HAPPENS BOOKS

There was a blood moon after sunset on the day Jesus was crucified, fulfilling Joel 2:31.
It has been verified by astronomical calculations to be April 3, 33 A.D.

69

The Beasts of Daniel and Revelation Explained
That are Already Nine-Tenths Here
By Douglas Wayne Ophus

It explains the ten locations of the seven kings with the antichrist having three locations and many of the things that will happen in the future.

70